TEEN MENTAL HEALTH™

cutting and
self-injury

Greg Roza

ROSEN
PUBLISHING®

New York

Published in 2014 by The Rosen Publishing Group, Inc.
29 East 21st Street, New York, NY 10010

First Edition

Library of Congress Cataloging-in-Publication Data

Roza, Greg.
Cutting and self-injury/Greg Roza.
    pages cm.–(Teen mental health)
Includes bibliographical references and index.
ISBN 978-1-4777-1750-9 (library binding)
1. Cutting (Self-mutilation)–Popular works. 2. Self-injurious behavior–Popular works. 3. Teenagers–Mental health–Popular works. I. Title.
RJ506.S44R69 2014
616.85'8200835–dc23

                                                              2013012404

Manufactured in the United States of America

CPSIA Compliance Information: Batch #W14YA: For further information, contact Rosen Publishing, New York, New York, at 1-800-237-9932.

contents

chapter one

What Is Self-Injury?

Have you ever been so depressed or sad that you thought about hurting yourself? Hopefully the answer is no, but you wouldn't be the only person to consider it. No matter who you are, everybody feels scared or sad from time to time, and people have difficulty dealing with emotional or stressful situations. Unfortunately, some people choose to injure themselves to deal with emotional pain. You may even know someone who has done this. How do you deal with stress and sadness?

During the Black Death plague of the mid-1300s, the flagellants whipped themselves in public, hoping to atone for everyone's sins.

Self-injury is deliberately inflicting pain on oneself, particularly if it results in tissue damage. Self-injury, believe it or not, is not usually a way to commit suicide. Rather, it's more often a cry for help.

Cutting and self-injury are behaviors that people have practiced for a long time. Beginning in the 1300s in Europe, groups of religious fanatics called flagellants beat themselves with whips to atone for their sins. They also did it during difficult times, such as droughts and plagues. The flagellants weren't trying to kill themselves; they were trying to replace one form of pain with another. They thought this was what God wanted, and they thought it would make things better.

Today, many teenagers self-injure themselves for similar reasons, thinking that physical pain will make other types of pain go away. People who self-injure themselves aren't trying to commit suicide, although their actions may seem suicidal to people close to them. Rather, they're trying to overcome mental or emotional pain—which is often difficult for young people to understand—with "real" physical pain.

A Rising Problem

Self-injury isn't a new phenomenon. However, thanks to the publicity it has gotten through television and movies, more people have become aware of self-injury in recent years, particularly cutting. Because of this, more and more kids have been turning to self-injury to cope with emotional problems. Current studies show that one out of twelve teenagers has deliberately self-injured themselves at least once.

The age of kids who self-injure themselves has also dropped recently. Karen Conterio is the founder of the treatment program SAFE (Self Abuse Finally Ends) and coauthor of *Bodily Harm: The Breakthrough Healing Program for Self-Injurers*. Conterio says that self-injury usually begins around age fourteen, but that in recent years kids as young as eleven have begun doing it. Many kids become aware of self-injuring behaviors as young as nine.

The following section will take a closer look at self-injury and the different forms it takes.

Cutting

Cutting has become one of the most popular forms of self-injury, but there are others as well, and each is just as dangerous as cutting. The information here might help you recognize the signs of self-injury in others. You may have seen people at school or the mall with random cuts on their arms. There's a chance they did it to themselves.

People who cut themselves on purpose aren't trying to cause deadly or even long-lasting injuries. Most of the cuts are small and shallow—just big enough to be hidden under long sleeves and pants. Some teens cut words and names into their skin. Some people cut themselves worse, often by accident.

People who cut themselves may practice other similar habits. They may bite their nails, rip skin from their fingers and lips, or pick old wounds open

Most cutters aren't trying to do serious harm, but accidents often lead to more lasting physical damage.

again. Some may rub or scrape their skin until it's raw. Others pull their own hair out. In some extreme cases, people who cut themselves may also embed sharp objects, particularly needles, in their flesh. Others have been known to swallow dangerous objects, such as pins and nails, which can do serious internal damage. While no form of cutting should be ignored, embedding and ingesting sharp objects is far more dangerous and often a sign of more serious problems.

Burning is another form of self-injury. Though they do it to their own bodies, people who burn themselves also risk setting fires and hurting others.

Burning

Instead of using sharp objects to harm themselves, some people use lighters or matches. Some like to see how long they can hold their hand over a flame until they can't take it anymore. Others may even touch a hot iron or stove. The results of burning are often very similar to that of cutting—small but noticeable injuries that can be hidden from parents and other adults.

A different version of burning is branding.

This is when a hot metal object is pressed against the skin. The resulting burn is bad enough to create permanent scar tissue. It doesn't help that some famous people, particularly athletes, often display artistic brandings on their arms.

Banging and Bruising

Very similar to cutting is bruising. People who do this may bang their forearms against a hard surface or punch their legs over and over. Sustained banging causes bruising. Others may bang their head against walls and lockers. Extreme cases of bruising and banging have led to broken bones.

Some consider bruising the "safe" form of self-injury because the injuries are more often mild, not to mention easier to explain to friends and family. Self-bruising may be easier to deny, but that doesn't make it any less dangerous than cutting or burning. As with any self-injuring behavior, there's an underlying illness that needs to be addressed.

Related Activities

The behaviors we've already talked about are sometimes found mixed with other potentially dangerous behaviors. The difference between these addictions and self-injury is that people who hurt themselves intend to do harm in the moment. Just because someone is experiencing conditions like those described here doesn't mean they're also cutting themselves. However, it's not uncommon to recognize these behaviors in someone who also practices self-harm.

People who injure themselves may also smoke and abuse drugs and alcohol. Some teens get addicted to huffing dangerous chemicals. People who self-medicate using legal and illegal drugs can become addicted to them, risking long-term damage and overdoses. Food-related problems such as anorexia, bulimia, and overeating often go hand-in-hand with self-injury. Risk-taking behaviors include dangerous stunts, reckless driving, breaking the law, and sexual promiscuity. Some even become addicted to fitness activities, driving themselves to extremes when it comes to working out or competing in sports.

What Do I Do?

Do you think you know someone who might be injuring him- or herself on purpose? With so many different types of self-injury and related behaviors, it can be difficult to diagnose. However, some signs are obvious, especially when they occur multiple times. This can be upsetting for those around people who self-injure, but it is often worse for the people injuring themselves. They have an underlying problem that needs to be addressed.

The information in this resource will help you better understand self-injury and cutting. For readers who fear someone they know is self-injuring themselves, it will help you decide if your friend is truly at risk of hurting him- or herself. For those of you who self-injure yourself, it can teach you how to reach out for help.

MYTHS AND FACTS

Myth: People who self-harm themselves are suicidal.

Fact: Self-injury is a method of coping with the stress caused by tragedy, depression, and other problems. However, people who injure themselves are usually not trying to commit suicide.

Myth: People who self-injure themselves are just looking for attention.

Fact: While many self-harming behaviors—such as cutting the arm or burning the palm with a lighter—are one-time events, many cases of self-injury mask more serious problems. People who harm themselves more often try to cover up the evidence rather than seek attention for it.

Myth: Since the cut, burn, or bruise isn't that bad, the problem must not be that bad.

Fact: Some people don't find cutting to be a serious problem. They think it's just teens being self-absorbed or destructive. No matter how small the wound, self-injury is often a sign of more serious issues.

Myth: Self-harm is something teens grow out of.

Fact: It's true that many teens "grow out of" self-injury, but that's usually because they find help, whether that's from a parent, friend, or doctor. Those who don't get help may find it difficult to stop. Some adults practice self-harming behaviors all their lives.

Myth: Cutters could just stop if they wanted to.

Fact: As with any addiction, it's hard for many teens to just stop. Some people need special help.

chapter two

Why Do People Injure Themselves?

Before we talk about why people injure themselves, we may want to answer the question "Who self-injures?" The general opinion, supported by formal studies, is that most cutters are female. However, it's not always easy to tell when someone is purposely harming himself or herself; some studies even show that males are equally likely to self-injure.

Self-injury isn't something that just happens to goth kids or loners. A fifteen-year-old athlete may practice self-harm, but so may a nineteen-year-old musician, or a twenty-year-old college student. Boys and girls, young and old—anyone can become addicted to self-harm in an effort to relieve stress, deal with tragedy, or just "feel alive."

Many people have a hard time understanding why someone would want to harm himself or herself on purpose, but the pain serves a basic biological function. The human body adapts to physical pain. It becomes a way to deal with confusing emotions. Self-harm may start as a one-time event, but just as with drug and alcohol abuse, it can become addictive. Most teens do it to replace one type of pain—physical, emotional, or mental—with

Parental fighting is a common cause of teen depression, which can lead to self-injury in some cases.

another pain. For cutters, the distress caused by over-whelming circumstances at home or at school can manifest as self-injurious behavior. Allowing this behavior to continue for too long can lead to worse problems.

Categorizing Self-Harm

When treating someone who has been harming himself or herself, identifying the cause of the behavior is the first step. Some serious mental illnesses—such as schizophrenia—are frequently accompanied by self-injury. However, the kinds of illness we're talking about are different. For most teenagers, self-injurious behavior is not a sign of mental illness. Rather it's a sign of impulsive behavior.

Psychiatrist and author Armando Favazza has developed a system for categorizing self-harm. This system includes four categories: stereotypic, major, compulsive, and impulsive. Stereotypic behaviors are repetitive movements (such as head banging) commonly seen in some forms of autism. Major self-injury, sometimes seen with patients suffering from psychotic disorders such as schizophrenia, can result in serious damage. Compulsive self-injury manifests as regular, often ritualistic self-mutilation. People who suffer from obsessive-compulsive disorder may feel compelled to cut themselves in a certain way on a regular basis to help alleviate real or imagined anxiety.

People who suffer from impulsive self-harm are different from individuals who practice the three forms discussed above. Teenagers who cut themselves to alleviate stress or just feel alive don't necessarily have a mental or developmental disorder. They know what they are doing and are aware of the results. Impulsive self-harm is caused by a number of biological, psychological, and social reasons.

Relieving Anxiety and Regaining Control

For many teens, self-injury is a method of coping with stress, loneliness, fear, depression, and other sources of anxiety. Feeling pain on the outside can block out or alleviate pain they feel on the inside. Many patients have described the moment of self-administered pain as a balloon popping. As they begin to cut them-selves, the anxiety drops, and they're left feeling more peaceful.

Overwhelming emotions such as those mentioned above can come from numerous sources. People suffering from intense feelings of guilt or shame may turn to self-injury as a form of self-punishment. Many teens who self-injure are victims of physical, mental, and sexual abuse in the home. Teens who are bullied may resort to cutting to help take their minds off of their problems. Stormy or failed relationships with friends and family can be overwhelming for young people, as well. Many teens aren't able to properly express their thoughts and emotions. Victims may suffer from feelings of self-hatred for having strong emotions and no way to express them. Self-harm becomes a way of getting rid of these feelings of helplessness and turmoil.

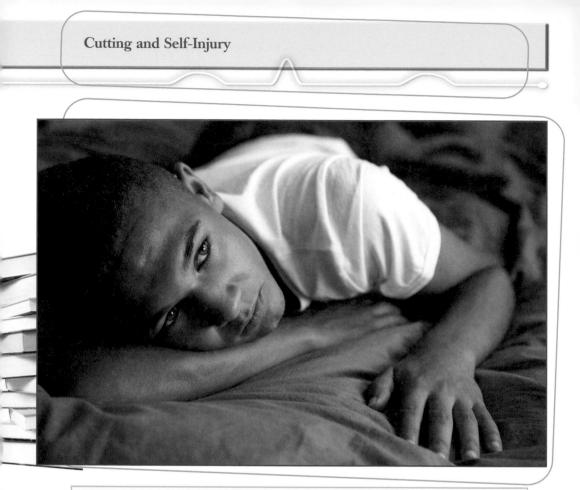

When you don't know how to cope with depression, it's hard to do just about anything, even get out of bed in the morning.

Feeling "Alive"

Some victims of self-mutilation feel disconnected from the world around them. They lack emotions and feel numb inside. Everyday life can be difficult in this frame of mind. Every action seems worthless, and nothing seems important or exciting.

Victims of parental neglect or abuse at a young age may ignore their emotions through dissociation, or

a detachment from their surroundings. Frequent and persistent cases of dissociation can even result in memory loss as the mind shuts out the world. Extreme cases of dissociation, often referred to as dissociative identity disorder, can result in split personalities and amnesia.

For people like this, a moment of pain caused by a cut or burn allows them to feel something. They lack the ability to feel emotions, so they fill that void with physical pain. The pain for them is both sobering and soothing.

Managing Pain

In some ways, self-injury is similar to drug and alcohol abuse. When the body is injured, the brain releases chemicals called endorphins. These substances help block pain and create feelings of relief and pleasure. This is very much like the euphoria people feel when they use drugs. Drugs and cutting are both used to help

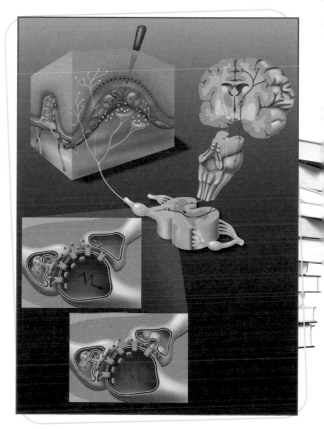

This image illustrates the "pain pathway" in the human body. This process triggers the release of endorphins.

alleviate emotional stress and to provide a temporary escape from emotional numbness.

If it's allowed to continue, using self-injury as a painkiller can lead to some very serious problems. Drug users often become used to the substances they abuse over time. It may take more of the drug to get the same sensation from it. This addictive behavior can lead to far worse problems, including accidental suicide when the person doesn't know how much is too much until it's too late. People who self-injure themselves can experience a similar scenario.

A self-injury high could last a few minutes, or it could last weeks. As someone hurts himself or herself more and more, the body may react differently. Some cutters start to feel like they need to hurt themselves more often to achieve the same sense of calmness or control. Others increase the severity of the injuries hoping for a greater rush from the endorphins. This can lead to more permanent skin tissue damage, or worse, to life-threatening wounds.

Communicating with Others

Many people try to hide their injuries. But you might be surprised to learn that some people use their injuries as a way of communicating with others. These people often have a hard time communicating in normal ways or haven't learned a healthier way of expressing their emotions. Or perhaps they've grown up feeling ignored or misunderstood.

Self-injury could be used to manipulate the feelings and actions of others. These actions are often fueled by anger and a desire to make others feel badly about their actions. For example, a teen might start cutting himself to "get even" with a neglectful parent. Another teen might do it to make her ex-boyfriend feel guilty for breaking up with her. On the other hand, some use self-injury in an attempt to drive others away from them.

For others, overt self-injury is a cry for help. Teens with neglectful parents may grow up feeling invisible and unreal. When parents don't know how to express their emotions, their children, too, fail to

When parents have a hard time expressing emotions in a healthy way, their children risk developing similar habits and behaviors.

develop appropriate coping skills. These teens are burdened with the feeling of being alone and voiceless. By cutting themselves, they aren't trying to be the center of attention. But they are trying to draw attention to themselves. They're hoping to be discovered by expressing how they feel about being ignored.

chapter three

The Signs of Self-Injury

The effects of self-injury show up in many ways. The most obvious symptoms involve tissue damage. Symptoms often look much like any common injury you might get during a typical day. Others injuries are more extreme, including deeper cuts, serious burns, and even broken bones. It's hard to miss injuries like that!

Others symptoms can be harder to identify. The obvious tissue damage is almost always the result of emotional problems, which are far more difficult to diagnose, especially for

teens. You might see a sudden change of mood or behavior, difficulty functioning at school or home, heightened levels of anxiety, and sometimes violent outbursts.

Regardless of whether it's a cause or an effect, self-injury is a clear sign that all is not well with a person and he or she needs help. It might be time to get the help of someone trained in self-injury therapy and treatment. Friends and family, however, are a crucial step in identifying self-injurious behavior and helping their loved one overcome it.

So, how can you recognize a symptom of self-harm? It's not always so easy. You may see small, regular cuts on a friend's hand and wonder how they got there. You might

Friends are often the first ones to see signs of self-harm in their peers. They can do a lot to help their friends get well.

notice that your brother always seems to have bruises on his arms. A close friend may suddenly become withdrawn and sad. Are these signs of self-injury? The answer is yes and no.

Just because someone you know shows one or a few of these symptoms doesn't mean this person is injuring himself or herself. However, knowing the signs and behaviors associated with self-harm will better prepare you to recognize the genuine problem if it ever happens to someone you know.

Physical Signs of Self-Injury

The immediate physical effects of self-harm depend on the individual method of injury. They include ordinary cuts, bruises, bumps, and burns. Not everyone you see with a minor injury is harming themselves on purpose. By paying close attention to the injuries, you may recognize ongoing patterns, which is a strong sign of self-injury.

Teens who cut don't always choose random ways to hurt themselves. The injuries often appear in regular shapes and patterns. The cuts on your friend's forearm may look too neat and straight. Sometimes they're lined up like railroad tracks. For some teens, injuring themselves becomes a routine, resulting in long-lasting and recurring wounds. Even the smallest cut has the potential to leave a scar. People who regularly cuts themselves are sure to have lasting marks on their bodies, something that will always remind them of a low point in their lives.

We've talked about the more obvious injuries, but some injuries may seem pretty strange to people who aren't familiar with self-harm. Some teens carve words into their skin—such as "loser," "fat," or random initials—which may be direct clues to their emotional problems. Some kids between the ages of five and thirteen suffer from an illness called trichotillomania. They feel an urge to twist and break their hair off, leaving bald patches. Some teens use ink and something sharp to draw crude tattoos on their bodies. This is particularly bad because tattoos last forever, unless they're removed by a specialist.

Look Around

Physical injuries might be plain to see, but you can learn something by observing a person's clothing as well. Teens with feelings of guilt, shame, and a fear of discovery often go to great lengths to hide their injuries. They might start wearing pants and long sleeves all the time, even in warm weather. Some might wear gloves, hats, or scarves at strange times. You may notice small blood stains on shirt sleeves or random drops of blood on clothing.

It's not a good idea to go snooping, but the objects in a person's room or locker at school or the objects they carry with them could be signs of self-injury. Cigarettes and lighters may be used to burn the skin. You may also find lit and unlit books of matches, which could be used to heat up metal objects. Razors, needles, and other random sharp objects (such as soda can tabs or broken glass) can be used to cut the skin. By looking around a person, and not just at him or her, you may find clues to the problem.

When you recognize that someone is purposely injuring himself or herself, it will probably seem like a sudden

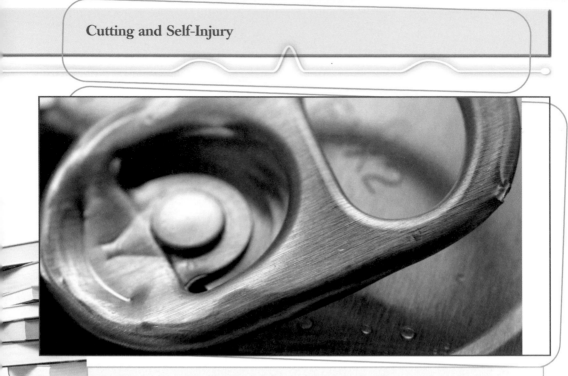

Even a seemingly harmless soda can tab can be sharp enough to cause bleeding. Unsanitary objects can also cause infection.

development. However, that's not always the case; it might be a long-lasting problem that you've just discovered. It might be easy to spot cuts and bruises, but it can be difficult to recognize the emotional warning signs. Parents, siblings, teachers, and friends need to watch out for the emotions that lead to self-injury and not just the injuries themselves.

Complications

The more often someone is cut, burned, or bruised, the greater his or her chances of developing more serious complications. After an extended period of self-harm, a teen might feel the need to increase the amount of pain inflicted to achieve the same sensation once felt. This can lead to a number of dangerous complications.

Someone who hides a particularly bad cut, one that might need stitches, runs the risk of blood loss and infection. Blood loss may also result from a misjudged cut that goes too deep. The same goes for burns. Infections result from using and reusing old or dirty objects, such as razors, scissors, nail clippers, and aluminum cans, to cut the skin. People who bang body parts can bruise themselves, but they can also cause broken bones and concussions. Without medical treatment, any of these injures could be life threatening.

Self-harm and prescription drug abuse often occur together. They're each used to escape feelings of depression and loneliness.

As we've already seen, self-harm can occur along with other dangerous behaviors and habits. People who injure themselves may also develop a drinking or drug problem. Some teens crave the thrill they get from dangerous stunts; thrill seekers may even practice self-harm openly. Teens who struggle with serious eating disorders often cut themselves in an act of self-punishment or self-loathing.

Though most people who practice self-mutilation don't want to kill themselves, when mixed with other dangerous activities, they increase their chances of doing just that.

Emotional Signs of Self-Injury

We've already talked about the emotions that people who intentionally hurt themselves experience—depression, anger, worry, fear, and many others. These are emotions that drive teens to self-injury in the first place. Teens risk entering a dangerous emotional cycle, as one illness feeds off another. Physical tissue damage leads to inner scars that can be harder to deal with.

Teens who cut themselves often have low self-esteem and difficulty dealing with feelings of sadness and anger. They may be depressed because of relationship problems or problems at home. As with other addictions, sudden mood changes associated with self-injury can be a clue as to what is going on. So are poor functioning at home, school, and work.

Be careful when trying to diagnose self-injury based on emotional criteria. It's safe to say that if someone you know is exhibiting any of the emotional problems mentioned here, he or she is in need of help. Without seeing evidence of cutting, burning, or bruising, it's not fair to think someone is committing self-injury. Take the time to talk to the person. Tell your friend that you're concerned and ask him or her to seek help from an adult. If you're sure self-injury is a problem, you should find an adult to help the person.

chapter four

Seeking Help and Getting Well

At the end of a sixteen-year British study, conducted in Australia, results showed that approximately one in twelve teenagers participated in self-harm at least once. The study showed that 10 percent of girls and 6 percent of boys admitted to committing self-harm. The good news is that a

Teachers and school counselors are often willing to help teens who are reluctant to turn to family members for help.

majority of these youths overcame self-harm, often by themselves. However, some teens required additional counseling and medical help to address their problems, a small percent of which included mental illnesses.

What can you do if you think someone you know is hurting himself or herself? Simply talking to the person shows you care. It also gives him or her the choice to start down the path to health and happiness. However, this isn't enough. You also need to notify an adult to ensure your friend gets help.

What can you do if it is you who suffers from self-injury? The first and most important step is to talk to someone—anyone. It could be a parent, grandparent, sibling, friend, teacher, coach, or priest. It doesn't matter who, just talk to someone you trust. This might prove to be the hardest step of all, but confiding in someone and

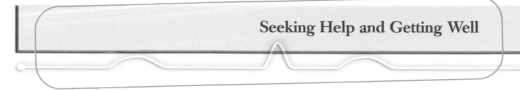

getting your problem out in the open will help start the healing process.

Friends and Family

The people closest to those who purposely injure themselves are almost always the first to notice the problem and can guide them in a healthy direction. Parents are among the first people to notice changes in mood and behavior. But in some cases, teens have neglectful or absent parents. The parents may in fact be the real reason the teen is hurting himself or herself in the first place. In instances like these, brothers and sisters may rely on each other for emotional support, but they, too, may be experiencing similar emotional problems. Who in your family are you close to? An aunt, uncle, or cousin might be able to help.

Close friends are sure to witness the mood shifts in someone's behavior, as well as the telltale signs of self-injury. What should you do? It's important to stay calm and in control. Your friend will likely come to you feeling depressed, scared, or angry. It's important to listen objectively without making judgments. You can offer to help your friend find help, but he or she may tell you to mind your own business. Whether your friend wants you to or not, it's your duty to notify an adult.

You may confide in a teacher with whom you are particularly close. School nurses, health teachers, and counselors are trained to deal with numerous students problems, including self-injury. People to whom you may be able to turn for help in the community include a scout leader, coach, or religious leader.

Mental Health Professionals

Once a case of self-injury is identified, several different types of mental health professionals might get involved. A teen's general practitioner or family doctor is a great place to start. Your doctor can discuss your illness with you and recommend a qualified specialist to help you.

Mental health counselors have been trained to give guidance with personal, social, or psychological problems. Most have one or more degrees, which could be in psychiatry, medicine, professional counseling, or education. Social workers have training in counseling, therapy, and mental health policy. They are trained to aid people, groups, and communities in overcoming social obstacles and improving

Your family doctor can give you advice about your health and your options for getting better, including a referral to an expert mental health professional.

their health and happiness. Psychiatrists are doctors of medicine trained to treat mental disorders. They can prescribe medications and conduct physical examinations and tests. Psychologists are similar kinds of doctors. However, their work is more often related to research and specialized testing rather than medical treatment.

Therapies for Self-Injury

Treatments, too, can vary based on the assessment of medical professionals. One of the most effective treatments is called dialectical behavioral therapy (DBT). Originally developed to treat a mental illness called borderline personality disorder, DBT has proved effective in

Group therapy can help show teens that they are not alone. They meet and talk with people their age who are dealing with similar problems.

helping teens accept themselves and giving them the tools they need to cope with negative feelings. Cognitive behavioral therapy (CBT) may be used to help an individual learn to recognize and address triggers that lead to self-injury. This helps teens learn how to better manage their emotions, thoughts, and behaviors. Both of these treatments entail multiple sessions with a trained professional as well as group therapy.

During psychotherapy, a therapist will help people figure out why they hurt themselves, paying close attention to the core emotional issues. Post-traumatic stress therapies may help teens with a history of abuse or incest. Hypnosis and other relaxation techniques may help reduce stress and anxiety and teach someone how to ease anxiety that precedes moments of self-injury.

Medications

Certain medications may help alleviate the negative emotions and conditions that go hand-in-hand with self-injury. Some medications are used to get someone well, painkillers for instance, and then they're discontinued. However, doctors and psychiatrists may suggest a long-term drug treatment plan. For example, some antidepressants, such as Zoloft and Prozac, have proved to be safe and effective for the continued treatment of depression and anxiety. These drugs treat negative moods by affecting the activity of neurotransmitters in the nervous system.

Mental Illnesses

In some instances, self-injury is a symptom of mental illness. A mental illness is a serious medical condition that disrupts thinking, emotions, moods, and behaviors and usually has a negative impact on everyday life. Mental illnesses for which self-injury is a symptom include autism, schizophrenia, Tourette's disorder, obsessive-compulsive disorder, and body dysmorphic disorder. Most mental illnesses are treated with various medications, counseling, and constant medical supervision.

Borderline personality disorder (BPD) is perhaps most often mistaken for self-injury, but it is far more serious. People with BPD experience long-term patterns of chaotic emotions and impulsive behavior. BPD can be hard to diagnose and treat because someone with this illness can live a normal life with a family and a job. However, they usually have a history of bad relationships, irrational anger, and emotional outbursts. They're also known to be highly impulsive. They may injure themselves without thinking about why they're doing it. For example, someone with BPD might punch walls or windows when angry, often resulting in broken walls and windows but also broken skin and bones. BPD is a mental illness treated with antidepressants and other drugs, as well as ongoing therapy and counseling.

Unlike BPD and other mental illnesses, most teens who commit self-harm do it for emotional reasons, not because they have a mental illness. This is not to say their problems aren't serious, but they can almost always be treated and cured by the professionals mentioned above. Some teens grow out of self-harm by themselves. People with mental illnesses, however, require long-term care and medication.

10

Great Questions to Ask A Mental Health Counselor

1. Which type of mental health professional can best help me?

2. Which method of treatment is best for me, and why?

3. Why can't I stop hurting myself? Is there an underlying problem?

4. Have you ever treated anyone who injures themselves?

5. How long do you think I will need to be in treatment?

6. Are there any medications that could help me? Are there alternatives to those medicines?

7. What can I do to manage stress in my life?

8. My parents won't listen to me. How can I get their attention without hurting myself?

9. Where can I find support groups to meet and talk to people like myself?

10. A friend of mine is cutting herself. What can I say or do to help her get better?

chapter five

Learning to Cope

Deciding to get better is a huge step in the right direction, but it's just the first step. Depending on the person, recovery can take weeks, months, or years; for most teens, self-injury treatment doesn't last that long. Some people make a break from self-injury and never look back. Others aren't so lucky. They may "revisit" cutting throughout their lives until they learn proper coping skills. Still others trade their self-injury addiction for other addictions, such as drugs and alcohol. A large portion of former self-injurers battle eating disorders.

People recovering from self-injury come to realize they are not helpless. By learning how to better interpret their emotions, and finding healthy alternatives to self-injury, anyone can overcome this harmful condition. It takes dedication to remain strong and stay healthy, but the effort is worth long-term happiness.

Help Yourself

Help from others when you have a problem with self-injury is very important. However, there are many steps

Writing your feelings in a journal helps make sense of complex emotions. It can help you recognize the triggers that make you want to hurt yourself.

you yourself can take if you want to get better. It's important to distance yourself from objects, activities, and people that trigger the desire to hurt yourself. Throw away the tools habitually used to cause harm, such as blades, pins, and lighters. Hang out with people who will support you and keep you company when you're feeling down. Keep a journal of your feelings and actions to help you figure out precisely what is wrong. Learn to avoid the negative emotions that lead you to hurt yourself and embrace more positive emotions and activities.

Once you are on the road to recovery, plan ahead to make your chances of total recovery even stronger. Research mental health therapists in your area who have considerable experience in treating self-injury. Get to know them to make sure they're a good match for you. They will let you know when they think you're ready to stop seeing them. Use the skills you learn in therapy to distance yourself from the triggers that lead to self-injury. Any good therapist or counselor will also be there for you in the future if you feel you need help.

Alternatives to Cutting

Former drug addicts often have cravings they must battle. The same goes for people who once had alcohol or eating problems. Self-injury is no different for many former addicts. Teens recovering from self-injury are taught to find healthy alternatives to cutting. Distraction is an effective way to cope with urges to harm yourself. Alternatives to cutting are numerous. You can narrow down your choices by asking yourself a few questions. What are your

Exercise is a great way to feel better and get in shape while distracting oneself from self-injury cravings.

skills and interests? Or is there something you've always wanted to learn but never found the time? Chances are good that you will find the perfect distraction.

Physical activities are perhaps the best way to distract yourself from urges or negative thoughts. Exercise forces you to concentrate on a single activity, and it allows you blow off steam at the same time. Imagine how therapeutic it would be to hit a punching bag for ten minutes! Joining a team sport may help you overcome a fear of being around others. Physical activity produces endorphins in the body very similar to the ones produced when people cut themselves, which is a much better way to receive a euphoric sensation. In short, exercise is beneficial to both physical and mental health.

Art, writing, and music are perfect alternatives to cutting. Sketching a landscape, singing along to a song on the radio, writing in a journal, playing the guitar, and many other artistic activities all provide a healthy way to express your thoughts, fears, and emotions.

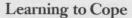

Sometimes, even the most basic chores or activities help chase urges away. Mowing the lawn, folding laundry, and sweeping the garage may not sound like fun, but simple activities like these help take your mind off negative thoughts. One person may find comfort in playing video games, while another may prefer building model cars. Some may even prefer to tear paper or break ice cubes. Take a walk. Call a friend. Write a poem. Read a book. It doesn't matter what the activity is, as long as it successfully helps you resist urges to hurt yourself.

Artistic activities can give depressed teens a positive outlet. Teens can also gain a better understanding of their emotions by exploring them through creative expression.

Support Groups

Support therapy is a regular part of many treatment programs, and it is often prescribed by medical professionals. But you can also find and join groups by yourself. You can ask your mental health professional to suggest a support group, or check the sources at the end of this resource.

In group therapy, teens struggling with self-injury meet others who are dealing with the same issues. They learn that they really aren't alone and that people of all ages and backgrounds are susceptible to self-injury. It's reassuring when other people share their thoughts and feelings in a group setting, allowing you to make connections with your own experiences. Hopefully, you might feel less ashamed of your problems and be able to speak about them openly to others who want to help. This will teach you healthy ways to express your emotions. It will also teach you how to stay positive and avoid negative thoughts and feelings.

You Can Do It!

The road forward may not always be easy. There will be times when the urge to hurt yourself will arise. You may not feel like you're strong enough to overcome negative thoughts and emotions. Or, you may not feel strong enough to help a loved one do the same. But you are strong enough, and you're not alone. Many others have battled self-injury and come out victorious. Now that you know more about self-injury, so can you. By becoming more attuned to your emotions and focusing on the positive things in life, you can look self-harm in the eyes and come away healthier, happier, and more confident than ever before.

autism A mental illness diagnosed in early childhood, marked by impaired social interaction and poor communication skills.

body dysmorphic disorder A mental condition marked by an excessive concern with a self-perceived physical defect.

cognitive Relating to the process of knowing or remembering something.

depression An emotional disorder marked by feelings of unhappiness, anxiety, and hopelessness.

dialectical Relating to discussion and reasoning.

disorder A medical condition involving a disturbance in the way the mind or body functions.

exacerbate To make a bad situation even worse.

huffing The practice of breathing in harmful chemicals in the hope of becoming inebriated.

mutilation The injury of a part of the body through cutting or removing flesh.

neurotransmitter A chemical that carries messages between different cells in the body.

obsessive-compulsive disorder An anxiety disorder marked by unwanted thoughts, worry, fear, and repetitive behaviors.

schizophrenia A serious mental illness characterized by hallucinations, delusions, and disorganized thoughts and behaviors.

Tourette's disorder A neurological disorder marked by repetitive, involuntary movements and vocalizations, called tics.

trigger An object, event, or person that causes the negative feelings associated with an addiction.

AMI-Québec
5253 Décarie Boulevard, Suite 200
Montreal, QC H3W 3C3
Canada
(514) 486-1448
Web site: http://www.amiquebec.org
AMI-Québec helps families manage the effects of mental
    illness through support, education, guidance, and
    advocacy.

Canadian Mental Health Association (CMHA)
595 Montreal Road, Suite 303
Ottawa, ON K1K 4L2
Canada
(613) 745-7750
Web site: http://www.cmha.ca
The CMHA focuses on combating mental health problems
    and emotional disorders.

The Cutting Edge
The Sidran Institute
200 E. Joppa Road, Suite 207
Towson, MD 21286
(410) 825-8888
Web site: http://www.sidran.org
The Cutting Edge is a newsletter about self-injury and is avail-
    able through the Sidran Institute, an organization that
    helps people who have experienced traumatic life events.

National Alliance on Mental Illness
3803 N. Fairfax Drive, Suite 100

Arlington, VA 22203
(703) 524-7600
Web site: http://www.nami.org
This organization is dedicated to improving the lives of
    Americans with mental illnesses. You can find informa-
    tion about support groups and educational programs.

National Institute of Mental Health (NIMH)
6001 Executive Boulevard
Rockville, MD 20852
(866) 615-6464
Web site: http://www.nimh.nih.gov
A federal health agency, the NIMH is the largest research
    organization specializing in mental health.

S.A.F.E. (Self-Abuse Finally Ends) Alternatives Program
40 Timberline Drive
Lemont, IL 60439
(800) DONTCUT (366-8288)
Web site: http://www.selfinjury.com
S.A.F.E. is one of the premiere organizations dedicated to
    helping self-injurers recover.

Self-Injury Foundation
P.O. Box 962
South Haven, MI 49090
(888) 962-6774
Web site: http://www.selfinjuryfoundation.org
The Self Injury Foundation provides funding for research
    in self-injury, as well as support and education for
    people affected by self-injury.

World Health Organization (WHO)
Avenue Appia 20
1211 Geneva 27
Switzerland
Web site: http://www.who.int
The WHO is the directing and coordinating authority of
the United Nations system concerned with interna-
tional public health.

Web Sites

Due to the changing nature of Internet links, Rosen
Publishing has developed an online list of Web sites
related to the subject of this book. This site is updated
regularly. Please use this link to access the list:

http://www.rosenlinks.com/TMH/Cutt

For Further Reading

Allman, Toney. *Self-Injury.* Detroit, MI: Lucent Books, 2011.

Carlson, Dale. *Addiction: The Brain Disease.* Madison, CT: Bick Publishing, 2010.

Cozic, Charles. *Teenage Mental Illness.* San Diego, CA: ReferencePoint Press, 2011.

Eagen, Rachel. *Cutting and Self-Injury.* New York, NY: Crabtree Publishing, 2011.

Farrell, Courtney. *Mental Disorders.* Edina, MN: ABDO, 2010.

Gratz, Kim L., and Alexander L. Chapman. *Freedom from Self-Harm.* Oakland, CA: New Harbinger, 2009.

Hollander, Michael. *Helping Teens Who Cut.* New York, NY: Guilford Press, 2008.

Hutchings, Melinda. *It Will Get Better: Finding Your Way Through Teen Issues.* Crows Nest, New South Wales, Australia: Inspired Living, 2010.

Hyman, Bruce M., and Cherry Pedrick. *Obsessive-Compulsive Disorder.* Minneapolis, MN: Twenty-First Century Books, 2011.

Ozer, Yvette Malamud. *A Student Guide to Health: Understanding the Facts, Trends, and Challenges.* Santa Barbara, CA: Greenwood, 2012.

Parks, Peggy J. *Self-Injury Disorder.* San Diego, CA: ReferencePoint Press, 2011.

Shapiro, Lawrence. *Stopping the Pain: A Workbook for Teens Who Cut and Self-Injure.* Oakland, CA: Instant Help Books, 2008.

Smolin, Lori A., and Mary B. Grosvenor. *Nutrition and Eating Disorders.* New York, NY: Chelsea House, 2011.

Williams, Mary E., ed. *Self-Injury.* Detroit, MI: Greenhaven Press, 2013.

Index

About the Author

Greg Roza has been writing and editing educational material for thirteen years and has written many books about health and well-being. Roza lives in Hamburg, New York, with his wife and three kids. Parenthood has taught him a lot about raising children and the problems they encounter growing up.

Photo Credits

Cover (right) © iStockphoto.com/abbywilcox; cover, p. 1 (top left inset) © iStockphoto.com/Matt_Brown; cover, p. 1 (middle left inset) © iStockphoto.com/LeoGrand; cover, p. 1 (bottom left inset) © iStockphoto.com/jane; cover, pp. 1, 3 (head and brain illustration) Yakobchuk; p. 3 (laptop) © iStockphoto.com/Colonel; pp. 4, 12, 20, 27, 35 (head and brain illustration) © iStockphoto.com/angelhell; p. 4 © iStockphoto.com/DRB Images, LLC; p. 5 Universal Images Group/Getty Images; p. 7 prudkov/Shutterstock.com; p. 8 WIN-Initiative/Getty Images; p. 12 © iStockphoto.com /alexxx1981; pp. 13, 24, 28 iStockphoto/Thinkstock; pp. 16, 30 Monkey Business Images/Shutterstock.com; p. 17 JACOPIN /BSIP/SuperStock; pp. 19, 25 SW Productions/Photodisc /Getty Images; p. 20 © iStockphoto.com/Juanmonino; p. 21 LeoGrand/E+/Getty Images; p. 27 © iStockphoto.com /nycshooter; p. 31 Zigy Kaluzny/Stone/Getty Images; p. 35 © iStockphoto.com/joshblake; p. 36 FineCollection/E+/Getty Images; p. 38 BananaStock/Thinkstock; p. 39 Chuck Rausin /Shutterstock.com; interior graphics (books) © iStockphoto .com/zoomstudio.

Designer: Nicole Russo; Editor: Nicholas Croce;
Photo Researcher: Karen Huang